FEARLESS: BREAKING FREE FROM ANXIETY'S GRIP

Allen Madding

Thomasville, GA

Ordering Information:
This book is distributed by Ingram, One Ingram Blvd., La Vergne, TN 37086. www.ingramcontent.com

Fearless: Breaking Free From Anxiety's Grip
by Allen Madding
ISBN 979-8-218-88381-2
Library of Congress Control Number: 2025926099

Table of Contents

4

Introduction

Fear and Anxiety are two extremely prevalent issues in our modern day culture with anxiety disorder ranking as the most common mental health condition globally.

According to the National Institute of Mental Health, almost a third of adults will experience an anxiety disorder at some point during their lives. (Mental Health Information, Statistics, Any Anxiety Disorder)

In 2024, the market for anxiety disorder treatment was $11.9 billion. It is estimated that it will reach $16.95 billion by 2034. (Anxiety Disorders Treatment Market Sizing, 2025)

God desires you to be free from all fear and anxiety. In the midst of overwhelming circumstances, He offers strength, courage, and hope. I invite you to look into His Word and discover His peace that passes all understanding. A peace that cannot be found in any other source.

It is the prayer of my heart that as you read this book, you encountered the healing power of God in your life to break the bondage of fear and anxiety. And that you experience freedom, restoration, and complete healing of your mind and spirit.

"Whatever [the] fears, encourage [yourself] to face them—and then turn them over to God. God loves [you], and when we know Christ and have put our faith and trust in Him, we know He'll never abandon us."
 - Billy Graham (10 Quotes from Billy Graham on Fear, 2020)

What's the Difference Between Fear and Anxiety?

Before we delve into each of these topics, lets first determine what the difference is between fear and anxiety. Where is the line of demarcation? How do we determine when we've crossed the line. What's the determining factor of differentiation?

Fear is focused on a specific and present perceived threat where anxiety has a much broader focus on future threats or uncertainties. Fear is typically much more sort-lived while anxiety can persist for longer periods even when there is no present threat.

Andres Felipe Sciolla, a professor of clinical psychiatry in the UC Davis Department of Psychiatry and Behavioral Sciences, describes the difference between fear and anxiety using elevators as an example.

"It would be normal to fear an elevator if you can see it is at maximum capacity or failing or shaking in a strange way." He explains. "Anxiety would be for someone to be afraid of an elevator even though it's a perfectly functional elevator, and you know it's been recently installed and checked, and yet you still have anxiety about using it." (Howard, 2023)

"Commit your life to Christ, and then when fears come, turn them over to God...Remember the Psalmist's words: 'The Lord is my light and my salvation — whom shall I fear? The Lord is the stronghold of my life — of whom shall I be afraid?' (Psalm 27:1)"

- Billy Graham (10 Quotes from Billy Graham on Fear, 2020)

What is Fear?

Merriam-Webster defines fear as "an unpleasant often strong emotion caused by anticipation or awareness of danger; an instance of this emotion; a state marked by this emotion" (Fear: Merriam-Webster)

Notice the definition says "an instance". It should be a brief experience that we overcome. Fear left unchecked can become excessive and paralyzing. Excessive fear can develop into a phobia or anxiety.

In Mark 5, as Jesus has just healed the woman with the issue of blood, someone runs up to the ruler of the synagogue to tell him that his daughter has died. Jesus hears the conversation and knows the man's natural reaction is an instant overwhelming fear and He speaks to it.

"Do not be afraid; only believe." Mark 5:36 NKJV

In that moment when grief and fear suddenly take us by surprise, He says "Don't fear! Just believe." Belief in the power and sovereignty of Jesus drives out fear. It can't exist in His presence. When the circumstances seem overwhelming, He is bigger! When we feel there's nothing we can do in the face of fear and we're afraid, He says *"Only believe!"*

When I was little, I had an overwhelming fear of free fall. So much so, that I often would suddenly wake up startled in the middle of the night having dreamed of falling - I could actually feel it! I was bound and determined to overcome that fear. My father was determined to see to it I overcame it as well. On a family trip to Six Flags Over Georgia, he convinced me to ride the brand new Great America Scream Machine. When we arrived to the park, I could see that massive white wooden rollercoaster from the parking lot. The train of cars flew down the 173ft tall hill of track at speeds reaching 68mph and around sweeping turns. It was colossal. Doubts and fear quickly entered my mind. I tried desperately to distract myself. We rode other rides including the smaller Dahlonega Mine train coaster that didn't seem so overwhelming. But the time came when Pop led me to the long queue line for the Great American Scream Machine. I began to hold my breath and the "What ifs" started running through my mind. Have you ever been overwhelmed with the "What ifs?" I was at that moment. As we entered the building that housed the queue line, there were rails on both sides of us, people to the front, people to the back. I felt like there was no escape. The fear got larger the closer we slowly approached the boarding platform. When we finally arrived at the final position and waited for the next train of cars, I turned to Pop and in a small trembling voice, I said "I don't think I can do this."

He looked down and me and laughed. "You ain't got no choice now, Son." He said. "You're already here."

He took my hand and led me to our appointed train car on the rollercoaster. We were quickly seated and the lap bar was ratcheted down in place. I can still remember the "clunk, clunk, clickity, clickity" sound as the cars slowly climbed the 173ft hill. As I grabbed the lap bar with all the strength my 12 yr old hands could muster, Pop encouraged me to look out at the expansive view - pointing out Stone Mountain in the distance, but I was focused on my breathing and my grip on that lap bar. And suddenly the event I had been dreading, we rolled over the top and began a rapid descent down the other side of that huge hill. As we gained speed, I became weightless. My butt rose from the seat until my thighs made contact with the lap bar. Images of me floating out of our car and falling down on the cars ahead began to run through my imagination. My knuckles turned white as I gripped the lap bar convinced I would plummet to my death if I lost grip. Finally, after what seemed like an eternity, we reached the bottom of the treacherous hill.

I hollered out to Pop, "You better hold on to me, my butt came off the seat on that big hill!"

As we raced thru curves and smaller hills, I began to breathe again. I calmed myself with the reassurance, the worst of it was over. As we exited our car at the loading platform, I walked on unsteady legs as I continued to recover from the experience.

I returned to Six Flags several time over the years, and I would get in line and ride the Great American Scream machine during every visit telling myself that I could do it, because I had survived it before. I graduated to the Great Gasp, a 225 ft tall parachute drop ride. I found that if I focused on the view from the top and tightened my abdominal muscles, I could withstand the momentary freefall. And you know what? I don't ever remember any more freefalling nightmares. I had faced that fear and conquered it. By returning and experiencing it over and

13

over again, I had overcome fear with familiarity and the knowledge that I had survived this in the past.

This is how we overcome fear in our lives. We face it head on instead of shirking away, we ask God, our heavenly Father, to hold on to us - and He is faithful to do it every time, and we continue in faith knowing that because He has carried us through other problems in the past, we know He will do it again. And just like that frightened little 12 year old boy at Six Flags, we conquer that fear and move on to face the next one.

In Matthew 14, the disciples are out on a boat headed towards Capernaum. They look up and Jesus is walking on the water towards them. At first they were frightened, and Jesus called out to them, *"It is I; do not be afraid."* Matthew 14:27 NKJV

So Peter thinks "that looks pretty nifty. I wanna give it a try!" He calls out to Jesus "if it's really you. Call me out and I'll come walk on the water with you." (my paraphrase, don't be offended.) So Jesus calls him out of the boat. Peter begins walking, but then he notices the waves are a little rougher than they looked from sitting in the boat. Fear grabs a hold of Peter, and he begins to sink. Immediately he cries out to Jesus, and Jesus stretches out His hands and righted him.

Jesus looks Peter in the eyes and says *"O you of little faith, why did you doubt?"* Matthew 14:31 NKJV

What happened to Peter is what happens to us. When we take our eyes off Jesus and focus instead on the size of our problems, fear rushes in to tell us the lies and sow seeds of doubt:

"You can't do it."

"You're too weak."

"You're ill equipped."

"You're not good enough."

"What if..."

The right response is to do just what Peter did. Cry out to Him and He will stretch out His arms and save us from the grips of our fear. "Don't doubt." He says "Trust Me. Have Faith."

In 1994, we were living in the rural Southwest Georgia where the owner of the local country store had been hounding me to volunteer with the community volunteer fire department. One evening I finally relented and attended one of their weekly meetings. When they found out I operated a business from our home and was in the district, they quickly gave me a radio even though I had not been through any training other than a walk around of one of the trucks and a brief tutorial on how to start the pump.

The next afternoon, I hear the department being dispatched to assist a neighboring community. I walked out to my truck and began to drive to the fire house thinking I would meet some of their seasoned volunteers and help however I could. Halfway to the firehouse, I heard the wife of the owner of the country store calling my number over the

15

radio with a sense of urgency to her voice. I quickly answered to learn no one else was in county, and she was ensuring I was responding. When I arrived at the firehouse, she ran across the dirt and gravel parking lot from the country store with some directions scribbled on a paper bag. I jumped in the fire engine and began trying to navigate my way to an unfamiliar area of the county. Over the radio, I could hear the frantic voice of a volunteer on scene.

"We need mutual aid from anyone available. It's a big, big fire!" He yelled.

When I finally arrived at the fire scene, it was pandemonium. A automotive shop was on fire. Neighbors were standing just a few feet from the fire watching. As I ran up to the single volunteer spraying water on the fire, paint cans were randomly exploding sending metal lids flying through the air.

"I'm out of water." He reported. "I gotta run to town to refill from a hydrant."

As he rolled up hose, jumped in his truck and departed, I ran back to our truck to find bunker gear, gloves, and a helmet. I was ill-prepared to be fighting a fire by myself, but something had to be done. As I was donning all the gear, the guy who had gave me the tutorial on the pump the night before came running up. It calmed my nerves a bit to know someone with experience was now alongside. I pulled hose, started the pump and backed him up on the nozzle as we made our initial attack on the fire.

About that time the shop's air compressor tank became over pressurized due to the exposure to heat setting off the tank's pop-off valve with a sudden heart-stopping BANG followed by a gushing of compressed air. I quickly realized what had happened as I tried to calm my breathing and slow my heart rate. I scanned the area to realize that all the spectators were gone. To this day, I don't have a clue where they went or how fast they ran. But one moment there was a deputy sheriff and about ten neighbors chatting away three or four feet from me, as we were engaging the flames. The next the two of us were completely alone with no one as far as the eye could see.

We had been fighting the fire for just a few minutes when he shut off the nozzle and instructed me to toss the hose down. Puzzled, I did as he ordered.

"I was getting shocked!" He explained.

As we turned and began examining the area, we realized the power lines that supplied the building had burned in two and were lying on the ground still energized. We had inadvertently drug the hose across them and the seeping water was producing an electric shock to the metal nozzle. We retreated to the safety of the fire engine while we waited for the utility company to disconnect the power and make the scene safe enough to re-engage the fire.

I learned a lot that day about the importance of ensuring scene safety, putting on all the gear before engaging a fire, crowd control, and fire fighting techniques. But more importantly, I learned about responding to the feeling of fear. I felt it. From the moment I pulled the fire engine up to the scene of a fully involved structure, the moment paint lids came flying over my head, the moment the air compressor tank vented, to the moment we almost got electrocuted, I had felt fear over and over. But what I learned that day was how to let it momentarily grab my attention and then push it down and not let it conquer me.

A lot of people look at firefighters and think "They're fearless!" Not at all. Firefighters feel the same fear that anyone else does. They've just learned to control it and not allow it to overcome them.

Make no mistake about it, we will always feel fear, but we don't have to be overcome by it. Courage isn't the absence of fear. Courage is moving forward and not allowing it to overtake you.

In First Samuel 17, we read the story of David and Goliath. Goliath was a giant around nine feet nine inches tall who had tormenting and scoffing at the troops of Israel for 40 days. When David arrived on scene to deliver food to his brothers and their army leaders, he was shocked to see the armies of Israel overcome with fear of the giant.

In verses 23-24, we read *"As he was talking with them, Goliath, the Philistine champion from Gath, stepped out from his lines and shouted his usual defiance, and David heard it. Whenever the Israelites saw the man, they all fled from him in great fear."* 1 Samuel 17:23-24 NIV

David is shocked that the armies of Israel are overcome with the fear of this giant hulking figure of a man.

"David asked the men standing near him, 'What will be done for the man who kills this Philistine and removes this disgrace from Israel? Who is this uncircumcised Philistine that he should defy the armies of the living God?'" 1 Samuel 17:26 NIV

I have no doubt that David could feel fear shake him when the nine feet 9 inch tall giant bellowed at them, but he refused to be overcome with fear like those troops that ran away. His response *"Who is this uncircumcised Philistine that he should defy the armies of the living God?"* David is saying, "I don't care how big that giant is. My God is bigger. I don't care how powerful that giant is, my God is more powerful!"

Don't believe me? Scroll down to verse 45.

David said to the Philistine, 'You come against me with sword and spear and javelin, but I come against you in the name of the Lord Almighty, the God of the armies of Israel, whom you have defied. This day the Lord will deliver you into my hands, and I'll strike you down and cut off your head. This very day I will give the carcasses of the Philistine army to the birds and the wild animals, and the whole world will know that there is a God in Israel. All those gathered here will know that it is not by sword or spear that the Lord saves; for the battle is the Lord's, and he will give all of you into our hands.'"
I Samuel 17:45-47 NIV

That should be our response to the giants that we encounter in our lives - divorce, cancer, job loss, death of a child or spouse - " *the battle is the Lord's.* " We will feel the fear,

19

but our God is greater and stronger. We have to face the feeling of fear and refuse to let it overcome us.

"Since Jesus overcame death, can He not help us overcome worry about the things that will probably never happen? We should turn worry into gratitude for all the times He has seen us through difficulties."
- Billy Graham (10 Quotes from Billy Graham on Fear, 2020)

What Does The Bible Say About Fear?

"There is no fear in love, but perfect love casts out fear. For fear has to do with punishment, and whoever fears has not been perfected in love." 1 John 4:18 NKJV

"The fear of man lays a snare, but whoever trusts in the Lord is safe." Proverbs 29:25 NKJV

The words "fear not" appear in the Bible over 60 times. At the end of this book, I've listed 61 scriptures that say "fear not." If He told us over 60 times, I don't think it's a suggestion or recommendation. I think it's a command. I'm pretty hard headed at times and sometimes I have to hear something a couple of times. Even for me 61 times highlights how important this subject is.

"For God gave us a spirit not of fear but of power and love and self-control." 2 Timothy 1:7 NKJV

"Therefore I remind you to stir up the gift of God which is in you through the laying on of my hands. For God has not given us a spirit of fear, but of power and of love and of a sound mind." 2 Timothy 1:6-7 NKJV

If God hasn't give us the spirit of fear, then who has? The enemy! Your enemy comes to kill, steal, and destroy.

"Be sober, be vigilant; because your adversary the devil walks about like a roaring lion, seeking whom he may devour." I Peter 5:8 NKJV

If we know fear is a spirit and it's a spirit of the enemy,

23

then we have to rebuke it and place it under our feet! Address the fear and command it to go in Jesus name!

Fear and anxiety is a means to sideline you from the plan God has for your life. You were created with purpose - a divine plan. You have a unique ministry that you are equipped to carry out. You have a unique set of giftings, talents, and abilities that you were given - a rare combination unlike anyone else. You were created with a specific purpose and the enemy is working as hard as possible to derail you from reaching that purpose. Fear and anxiety are one of the lies the enemy tries to utilize to divert you from the plan God has for you.

The good news is, God is more powerful. He is more able. He can break the grip of fear and anxiety in your life and empower you to achieve more than you have ever imagined.

"Fear not, for I am with you; be not dismayed, for I am your God; I will strengthen you, I will help you, I will uphold you with my righteous right hand."
Isaiah 41:10 NJKV

"For I, the Lord your God, will hold your right hand, Saying to you, 'Fear not, I will help you.'"
Isaiah 41:13 NKJV

"Have I not commanded you? Be strong and courageous. Do not be frightened, and do not be dismayed, for the Lord your God is with you wherever you go."
Joshua 1:9 NKJV

"I sought the Lord, and he answered me and delivered me from all my fears." Psalm 34:4 NKJV

You cannot overcome fear and anxiety on your own, but you can through the strength provided by God. He promises to strengthen you and uphold you. He promises to help you. Read those two verses over and over. Commit them to memory. God's promises are YES and AMEN. His Word says so!

"For no matter how many promises God has made, they are 'Yes' in Christ. And so through him the 'Amen' is spoken by us to the glory of God." 2 Corinthians 1:20 NIV

"Amen" comes from the Hebrew word "'āmēn," which means "truth" or "certainty." It is often equated to saying "So Be It!" It is one word that says "I trust God's will and promises!"

Claim those promises in your life. Whenever you feel doubt creeping in - whenever you begin to think that you cannot overcome fear's grip, read those verses out loud and say "God has promised me that He will provide me the strength to overcome fear!"

"Every tomorrow has two handles. We can take hold of it with the handle of anxiety or the handle of faith. We should live for the future, and yet should find our life in the fidelities of the present; the last is only the method of the first."
- Henry Ward Beecher (1813–1887)

What is Anxiety?

At one time or another each of us has experienced anxiety - a feeling of fear, dread, and uneasiness. You might begin to sweat, you might feel restless and tense, and you might experience a rapid heartbeat. Left unchecked, it can begin to negatively impact your job performance, your school work, and your relationships. In its extreme forms, anxiety is a fixation on ordinary issues like money, work, family, and health.

Towards Healthcare provides this definition, *"Anxiety disorders are mental health conditions marked by excessive worry, fear, or nervousness that can mess with daily life. They come in various forms like generalized anxiety disorder, panic disorder, social anxiety disorder, and specific phobias. People with these disorders often worry too much, even when there's no real reason. They might also experience physical symptoms like sweating, trembling, or rapid heartbeat. Some may avoid situations that trigger anxiety, leading to isolation or disruption of normal activities. Panic attacks, sudden and intense episodes of fear, are common, bringing along symptoms such as chest pain or difficulty breathing. Sleep troubles are another hallmark, with insomnia or racing thoughts making it hard to rest."* (Anxiety Disorders Treatment Market Sizing, 2025)

According to the National Institute of Mental Health (NIMH), over 40 million (19.1%) of US adults have an anxiety disorder. The World Health Organization (WHO) reports that anxiety is the world's most common mental disorder affecting 301 million people worldwide.

Anxiety is a by-product of our body's natural instinct of "fight-or-flight" which signals the brain to release a host of chemicals - hormones epinephrine (adrenaline) and norepinephrine (noradrenaline), and cortisol that increases our heart rate, our breathing, and our blood flow to muscles to prepare for immediate action to ensure our survival. This is a wonderful natural response in crisis situations where we are threatened with death or bodily harm, however the mind and body react to both actual threats and perceived threats. The reaction to false alarms and irrational fears are when it becomes an issue that requires addressing.

Anxiety left unaddressed causes physical damage such as cardiovascular disease and high blood pressure, and leads to irritability causing damage to relationships - we hurt those closest to us. Additionally, unaddressed anxiety leads to depression and seeking unhealthy ways of coping such as alcohol and drugs. Anxiety coupled with depression increase the risk of suicide. Anxiety cannot be left alone to run its course!

I won't pretend that my bouts with anxiety can even compare to what many people experience. I can only share my experiences with it. Heavy traffic and crowds can kick off anxiety within me. It seems odd when I think about it, because I lived in the Atlanta and Tampa metro areas for several years and adjusted to driving I-75, I-285, GA400, I-275, and I-4 on a regular basis. But there have been times when I have wrestled with traffic to get to the grocery store and it seems like everyone is trying to run me over in the parking lot, and then inside the store. All of a sudden I'm jumpy, my heart is racing, and I feel like I need to run. There have been times I've told my wife, I have to go to the truck. And I have to go out to the parking lot, recline the seat, put on some slow soft jazz, and try to settle my nerves. I've seen it creep up in crowded parks where people are bumping into me, pushing, and shoving. Suddenly, I either have to find a quiet place to go sit, or we have to leave. Thankfully Disney World has the boats that slowly go from one park to another, air conditioned shows, and Disney Skyliner cable cars where I can escape the maddening throng of people and recompose.

I've recognized the signs and symptoms, and I've realized it occurs more frequently when I am tired. So, I've tried to make sure that when I begin to get tired and I am in crowded venues or heavy traffic, that I take a break and remove myself from the situation that is causing the reaction for a little while. But I don't allow myself to isolate from going to amusement parks or concerts, because I refuse to let it take control of my life. When it rears its ugly head, I began to pray - focus on Jesus and denounce the anxious thoughts, slow my breathing, and repeat to myself *"Be still and know I am God."* Psalm 46:10 NIV

The good news is that the God who created you, loves you, and sees value and purpose in your life does not want you dealing with anxiety!

"Do not be anxious about anything, but in every situation, by prayer and petition, with thanksgiving, present your requests to God." Philippians 4:6 NIV

When you begin to experience the symptoms of anxiety creeping up into your daily life (panic, dread, uneasiness, irritability, feeling on the edge, obsessive thoughts, difficulty concentrating, shortness of breath, heart palpitations, sweaty hands, insomnia):

- Pause!
- Take a deep breath through your nose. hold it for 5 seconds. Slowly exhale through your mouth.
- Close your eyes and picture a tranquil scene (the waves crashing on the beach on a beautiful day, an eagle gliding through the air over a snow capped mountain, a deer drinking water from a creek in the forest)
- Begin to pray and denounce the spirit of fear. Claim God's Word over your life.
- Identify 3 things you are grateful for and Thank God for those 3 things

"Anxiety weighs down the heart, but a kind word cheers it up." Proverbs 12:25 NIV

You don't have to wait for someone else to provide a kind word. Speak kindly to yourself. The enemy wants you to listen to lies like you're not good enough, you're too messed up, you always mess up, etc. Battle that daily by speaking kindly to yourself.

"I am a chosen child of God!"

"I am beautifully and wonderfully made."

"I was created with a divine purpose."

"The God of all creation created me. and sacrificed his own innocent son on my behalf."

You cannot carry the weight of this life. You cannot solve the problems you are facing. God can! He can overcome anything you face by the power of the Holy Spirit within you. But you have to totally surrender to His will and power. You have to submit to His will. You have to come to the place that you lay it down.

"Cast all your anxiety on him because he cares for you."
1 Peter 5:7 NIV

When anxiety comes knocking and you feel overwhelmed, tell Him!

"God I cannot deal with this. This is more than I can handle on my own. I need you right here, right now. I'm trusting you with this problem and this situation. You are all wise and all powerful. Only you can overcome this problem. I trust you with it."

"God cannot give us a happiness and peace apart from Himself, because it is not there. There is no such thing."
C.S. Lewis (Lewis, 2001)

What is Peace?

Peace is a learned set of skills for remaining unaffected by a problem. Peace is NOT the absences of problems.

"Oh that sounds good on the surface, but how in the world do you expect me to by unaffected by the problem?"

Good question!

We achieve peace by recognizing that we are not in control. Control is trusting yourself and the illusion that you can fix everything. We interrupt this program to bring you this late breaking news: You cannot fix everything! You can't fix cancer. You can't fix the death of a child, parent, or loved one.

Good news: Peace does not come from being in control.

"Trust in the Lord with all your heart and lean not on your own understanding; in all your ways submit to him, and he will make your paths straight. Do not be wise in your own eyes; fear the Lord and shun evil. This will bring health to your body and nourishment to your bones". Proverbs 3:5-8 NIV

When we trust in God and recognize that He (not we) is in control, we can achieve peace.

"What does that mean?"

Glad you asked!

First, trust God's Word recorded in the Bible is true.

"For the word of the Lord is right and true; He is faithful in all he does. The Lord loves righteousness and justice; the earth is full of his unfailing love." Psalm 33:4-5 NIV

Second, trust that all of God's promises are true.

"God is faithful, who has called you into fellowship with his Son, Jesus Christ our Lord." 1 Corinthians 1:9 NIV

"For no matter how many promises God has made, they are "Yes" in Christ. And so through him the "Amen" is spoken by us to the glory of God." 2 Corinthians 1:20 NIV

Third, trust that God loves you and wants the absolute best for you.

"For I am convinced that neither death nor life, neither angels nor demons, neither the present nor the future, nor any powers, 39 neither height nor depth, nor anything else in all creation, will be able to separate us from the love of God that is in Christ Jesus our Lord." Romans 8:38-39 NIV

"For God so loved the world that he gave his one and only Son, that whoever believes in him shall not perish but have eternal life." John 3:16 NIV

"Whoever does not love does not know God, because God is love." 1 John 4:8 NIV

"And so we know and rely on the love God has for us. God is love. Whoever lives in love lives in God, and God in them." 1 John 4:16 NIV

"The Lord is compassionate and gracious, slow to anger, abounding in love." Psalm 103:8 NIV

"What, then, shall we say in response to these things? If God is for us, who can be against us?" Romans 8:31 NIV

What happens in life is: We get caught up in the current struggle and problem that we are facing and cannot see the bigger picture. We are down here playing checkers and God is playing chess. When you go to the doctor with a bad cut, the first thing they have to do is clean the wound. And the act of cleaning the wound hurts. We get so focused on the hurt and that hurt isn't good that we lose focus that it is a requirement to start the healing journey.

God isn't trying to help you create your peace. He is trying to GIVE you His peace - a peace that passes ALL understanding!

"Peace I leave with you; my peace I give you. I do not give to you as the world gives. Do not let your hearts be troubled and do not be afraid." John 14:27 NIV

" Be anxious for nothing, but in everything by prayer and supplication, with thanksgiving, let your requests be made known to God; and the peace of God, which surpasses all understanding, will guard your hearts and minds through Christ Jesus." Philippians 4:6-7 NKJV

The Message version says it this way: *"Don't fret or worry. Instead of worrying, pray. Let petitions and praises shape your worries into prayers, letting God know your concerns. Before you know it, a sense of God's wholeness, everything coming together for good, will come and settle you down. It's wonderful what happens when Christ displaces worry at the center of your life."*

Receiving God's Peace

Here are three steps for reordering our lives to receive God's peace:

Plan For Peace
"Careful planning puts you ahead in the long run; hurry and scurry puts you further behind". Proverbs 21:5 The Message (MSG)

"Do What?"

Yes. You have to plan and be intentional to receive peace. Take time away from "peace drainers". You know those people, places, or activities that seem to suck every ounce of peace you might have.

Practice Peace
"Do not be anxious about anything, but in every situation, by prayer and petition, with thanksgiving, present your requests to God. And the peace of God, which transcends all understanding, will guard your hearts and your minds in Christ Jesus." Philippians 4:6-7 NIV

By praying about every situation that comes up, we submit that we have no control over the situation and acknowledge that God does. Peace comes when we rest in the knowledge that God has us and He is working all things for our best interest.

"... by prayer and petition, with thanksgiving..." an unthankful heart is an entitled heart. Stopping in the midst

of the storm and listing the things in our lives that we can be thankful for helps us recognize that God is good, what He has provided for us and done for us in the past, and opens our hearts and minds for the possibilities of what He can do with this situation.

Protect Your Peace

If you spend any time talking with me, you might come to the conclusion that I am a marketing representative for the book "Boundaries" by Cloud and Townsend. Let me tell you I am not under their employ or under their publisher's employ. But if I can recommend one book after the Bible that has done more for me in healing and coping with relationships, "Boundaries" would be that book. I constantly search for copies of it in used book stores and yard sales and give them away like AOL used to give away CDs (dating myself there). My grandfather once said "Fences make for good neighbors." The older I get the more I appreciate the wisdom in that simple statement, and it directly applies to relationships. Building walls and shutting people out is our natural "flesh" reaction, but isn't the right solution for dealing with people that drain our peace. However building fences is quite healthy. When we build a fence, we can walk over to the fence and have a conversation over the fence with a neighbor. But we don't let everyone in our yard and into our home. With fences, we build gates and we get to decide who we let in the gate and who we do not. So we create a bit of distance where we can be cordial and engaged, but we don't have them in our living room for hours on end if we know they drain our peace. The fence allows us to have time and space constraints around our interactions with those individuals.

For years, I tried to have a level of relationship that was unachievable with a family member who was a peace drainer. Out of guilt, I continued to beat my head against a brick wall trying to have long interactions and a deep level of relationship that was unattainable and inevitably would melt down into a complete disaster. What I eventually learned is that we could have healthy interactions for a finite amount of time with limits. But I could not get in a car and drive 12 hours with them and expect things not to go off the rails. It just wasn't possible. I was introduced to the Boundaries book by Henry Cloud and John Townsend several years ago in a study while attending the Atlanta Vineyard. What I found was I needed to learn to create boundaries or construct fences in all my relationships. I couldn't continue in my idealist approach that everyone I met was someone I could have a deep meaningful relationship. I needed to exercise some restraint in who I let through the proverbial gate in my fence, into my yard, and eventually into my house. Some relationships will stay on the other side of the fence forever and that is fine. Some will be allowed to enter the yard but not the house. Some will need to be re-evaluated as life happens. Some will need to have their access revoked and put back on the outside of the fence.

If you are struggling with peace drainers in your life, I highly recommend getting yourself a copy of Boundaries and really dig into it.

"Let the peace of Christ rule in your hearts, since as members of one body you were called to peace. And be thankful." Colossians 3:15 NIV

"You will keep in perfect peace those whose minds are steadfast, because they trust in you." Isaiah 26:3 NIV

How to Overcome

First, recognize and identify the lies the enemy is telling you. The enemy is feeding you lies. You hear these lies in your thoughts every day. As Joyce Meyers demonstrates in her book, *Battlefield of the Mind*, our thoughts are where we both hear from God and from the enemy. Test every thought that enters your mind against the Word of God. If it lines up with scripture, you can trust God is speaking to you. If the thought doesn't line up with the Word of God, then it's the father of lies speaking to you.

" ...He was a murderer from the beginning, not holding to the truth, for there is no truth in him. When he lies, he speaks his native language, for he is a liar and the father of lies. " John 8:44 NIV

Recognize the lies and replace them with the truth, because the truth will set you free!

"...Jesus said, 'If you hold to my teaching, you are really my disciples. Then you will know the truth, and the truth will set you free.'" John 8:31-32 NIV

The Lies vs. the Truth

Lie: You are alone

Truth: *"Then the eleven disciples went to Galilee, to the mountain where Jesus had told them to go. When they saw him, they worshiped him; but some doubted. Then Jesus came to them and said, 'All authority in heaven and*

43

on earth has been given to me. Therefore go and make disciples of all nations, baptizing them in the name of the Father and of the Son and of the Holy Spirit, and teaching them to obey everything I have commanded you. <u>*And surely I am with you always, to the very end of the*</u> <u>*age.'"*</u> Matthew 20: 16-20 NIV

Lie: You are not worthy of love

Truth: *"But God demonstrates his own love for us in this: While we were still sinners, Christ died for us."* Romans 5:8 NIV

" for all have sinned and fall short of the glory of God, and all are justified freely by his grace through the redemption that came by Christ Jesus." Romans 3:23-24 NIV

"Are not five sparrows sold for two pennies? Yet not one of them is forgotten by God. Indeed, the very hairs of your head are all numbered. Don't be afraid; you are worth more than many sparrows." Luke 12:6-7 NIV
It's so important that you grasp your worth, God had this written this message twice in the Bible. It's in Matthew as well:
*" Are not two sparrows sold for a penny? Yet not one of them will fall to the ground outside your Father's care. And even the very hairs of your head are all numbered. So don't be afraid; you are worth more than many sparrows."*Matthew 10:29-31 NIV
If He had it recorded twice, He's stressing the worth He sees in your life!

You bear the image of God himself. That in itself demonstrates your value!
"So God created mankind in his own image, in the image of God he created them; male and female he created them." Genesis 1:27 NIV

At the end of the day, God reviewed everything he created (including YOU) and said it was good - not only good, but VERY good!
"God saw all that he had made, and it was very good. And there was evening, and there was morning—the sixth day." Genesis 1:31 NIV

"For you created my inmost being; you knit me together in my mother's womb. I praise you because I am fearfully and wonderfully made; your works are wonderful, I know that full well." Psalm 139:13-14 NIV

Lie: You are not enough

Truth: We don't have to survive this world in our own strength. God provides our power and strength. My His power and His strength, we can overcome anything!

"So do not fear, for I am with you; do not be dismayed, for I am your God. I will strengthen you and help you; I will uphold you with my righteous right hand." Isaiah 41:10 NIV

"I can do all this through him who gives me strength". Philippians 4:13 NIV

"But he said to me, "My grace is sufficient for you, for my power is made perfect in weakness." Therefore I will

boast all the more gladly about my weaknesses, so that Christ's power may rest on me." 2 Corinthians 12:9 NIV

"It is God who arms me with strength and keeps my way secure." 2 Samuel 22:33 NIV

"The Lord is my strength and my shield; my heart trusts in him, and he helps me. My heart leaps for joy, and with my song I praise him." Psalm 28:7 NIV

"The Lord is my strength and my defense]; he has become my salvation. He is my God, and I will praise him, my father's God, and I will exalt him." Exodus 15:2 NIV

" He gives strength to the weary and increases the power of the weak." Isaiah 40:29 NIV

Lie: God can't forgive the stuff you've done. You're way beyond forgiveness

Truth: God's love and forgiveness for you knows no limits!

"If we confess our sins, he is faithful and just and will forgive us our sins and purify us from all unrighteousness." 1 John 1:9 NIV

" My dear children, I write this to you so that you will not sin. But if anybody does sin, we have an advocate with the Father—Jesus Christ, the Righteous One. 2 He is the atoning sacrifice for our sins, and not only for ours but also for the sins of the whole world." 1 John 2:1-2 NIV

"He does not treat us as our sins deserve or repay us according to our iniquities. For as high as the heavens are above the earth, so great is his love for those who fear him; as far as the east is from the west, so far has he removed our transgressions from us. As a father has compassion on his children, so the Lord has compassion on those who fear him; for he knows how we are formed, he remembers that we are dust." Psalm 103:10-14 NIV

"You see, at just the right time, when we were still powerless, Christ died for the ungodly. Very rarely will anyone die for a righteous person, though for a good person someone might possibly dare to die. But God demonstrates his own love for us in this: While we were still sinners, Christ died for us." Romans 5:6-8 NIV

"I urge, then, first of all, that petitions, prayers, intercession and thanksgiving be made for all people for kings and all those in authority, that we may live peaceful and quiet lives in all godliness and holiness. This is good, and pleases God our Savior, who wants all people to be saved and to come to a knowledge of the truth."
1 Timothy 2:1-4 NIV

See that? Don't miss it. He wants ALL people to be saved and know the truth! All people, everyone - even you!

Lie: God can never use you because of your past

Truth: God can use your past. Your mess is a message. Your journey is a testimony of the goodness of God. What He has brought you through demonstrates His power and ability to bring someone else through similar circumstances.

Have you ever heard the story of Saul? He was a Roman citizen whose Hebrew name was Saul which in Latin was Paul. Saul was a Pharisee - a member of an ancient Jewish sect who were noted for their strict obedience of oral tradition and written law to the extent that they were criticized for focusing on external practices and traditions more than authentic faith. He actively persecuted early Christians for their beliefs. You find him introduced at the stoning of Stephen in Acts 8:1-3 where he approved of the Sanhedrin - the Jewish high court killing Stephen.

On the road to Damascus to arrest a group of Christians, Saul was blinded by a bright light and heard Jesus speak to him.

"Meanwhile, Saul was still breathing out murderous threats against the Lord's disciples. He went to the high priest and asked him for letters to the synagogues in Damascus, so that if he found any there who belonged to the Way, whether men or women, he might take them as prisoners to Jerusalem. As he neared Damascus on his journey, suddenly a light from heaven flashed around

him. He fell to the ground and heard a voice say to him, 'Saul, Saul, why do you persecute me?'

'Who are you, Lord?' Saul asked.

'I am Jesus, whom you are persecuting,' he replied. 'Now get up and go into the city, and you will be told what you must do.'

The men traveling with Saul stood there speechless; they heard the sound but did not see anyone. Saul got up from the ground, but when he opened his eyes he could see nothing. So they led him by the hand into Damascus. For three days he was blind, and did not eat or drink anything." Acts 9:1-9 NIV

Later in verse 18, Saul is healed by Ananias, one of the Christians that Saul was headed to persecute. He was baptized and began proclaiming the gospel. He was eventually responsible for spreading the gospel in Asia Minor and Europe. It is believed that he is the author of 14 of the 27 books in the New Testament. It is an undisputed fact that he wrote 7 of them.

If God could used Saul/Paul who persecuted and oversaw the killing of the early Christians, He certainly can use you.

"For we are God's handiwork, created in Christ Jesus to do good works, which God prepared in advance for us to do." Ephesians 2:10 NIV

It is what you were created to do!

Change What You're Doing

Dr. John Delony, a mental health expert with two PHDs, offers 11 steps in addressing anxiety (Delany, 2025):

1. Stop being alone.
2. Take a deep breath and drop your shoulders.
3. Turn off the news.
4. Write down your thoughts.
5. Go outside.
6. Move your body.
7. Back off caffeine, alcohol and sugar.
8. Rest.
9. Start a gratitude journal.
10. Eat real food.
11. Make a to-do list—and schedule margin.

That list looks pretty simple at first blush, but let's consider what he is recommending. Loneliness and isolation is unhealthy. Right now as you read that, a little voice inside your head is saying "I don't need anyone. I don't need people. People have failed me." And that little voice is telling you lies. Isolation and separation is where the enemy wants us. Where there isn't anyone else speaking truth and checking us when stinking thinking creeps into our thought processes.

"Stop being alone"
Whether you realize it or not, you go through your day with two voices in your head speaking thoughts. Without carefully evaluating these voices, you probably think "Oh, that's just me." One voice in your thoughts is God quietly

speaking truth and direction. The other voice is the enemy speaking empty lies. God says "community is good." The enemy says "You don't need anyone. You're better all alone." How do we tell the two apart and begin to listen to the right voice? Test your thoughts against the Word of God. Check your thoughts against the Bible. I often say if a thought seems too pure, too innocent, too good for anything that I would come up with - it's probably God!

Avoid the temptation to walk through life's journey alone. Fight the urge to stay alone! You need friends to walk alongside you and help you check bad attitudes and when you're getting off the right path.

"Take a deep breath and drop your shoulders"
What's the first thing you automatically do when you're frightened? Quickly inhale and hold our breath! which cuts off the oxygen to our brain and hinders the thought process. Feeling anxious? Relax by concentrating on slowing your breathing. Concentrate on slowly inhaling through your nose, holding it for a couple seconds, and then releasing the breath out your mouth.

"Turn off the news"
This one is my biggest pet peeve. Here's a news flash: Walter Cronkite is dead. The old days of unbiased news are gone. What we have today is propaganda networks. There I said it. There are two political biases and every TV and radio network subscribes to one side or the other. The networks are providing you an unbiased account of world events. The networks are providing you their slant or their take on the world's events. And no matter which side your

listening to, the end result is the same - doom and gloom. Watching and listening to the news is depressing. Turn it off.

"Write down your thoughts"

Oh boy! This is a struggle especially for us men. But what we don't realize is that we can get caught in a loop of worry and over thinking. When we write down our thoughts and then begin reading it, it becomes easier to carefully review our thoughts and find the over exaggeration and pick out the truth. I'm not going to tell you that you need to pledge to journaling your thoughts every day for the rest of your life. But I will suggest that you try it for a week or so, and see if it helps you to begin to identify the two voices and to discern which one is speaking truth and which one is speaking lies.

"Go outside"

Go for a walk. Get out of your routine and change your focus. Look at the trees, the flowers, the squirrels, and the birds. Listen to the birds, crickets, and frogs. Take in the beauty of creation. It will bring a tranquil feeling of peace and calm.

A Word of Encouragement

Let me encourage you. If you battle anxiety, do not let the accuser of the brethren saddle you with guilt. Anxiety is a shared human struggle. Do not let fear or shame keep you from seeking assistance in overcoming anxiety. Your journey to overcoming anxiety can require a combination of self-care, Christian counseling, medical treatment, and spiritual support from pastoral care and the community of faith. Do not dismiss a crucial element of your triumph over anxiety.

Consider Christian Counseling

Do not hesitate to seek counseling. Christian counseling is an extremely helpful tool in conquering anxiety. Christian counseling can provide a safe and non-judgmental environment to discuss and process thoughts and fears with trained counselors who offer support, empathy, compassion, hope, and encouragement. Christian therapy isn't just about treating anxiety in a clinical sense — it's about looking at the whole person, mind, body, and spirit. What makes it so powerful is that it brings faith into the process, so you're not just learning coping techniques, you're also grounding yourself in something bigger than the anxiety itself. For many people, that means finding peace in prayer, strength in scripture, and comfort in knowing they're supported both emotionally and spiritually. It's a holistic approach that doesn't separate mental health from faith, and that combination can be incredibly reassuring when life feels overwhelming.

Consult a Physician

Also, do not neglect pursuing consulting a physician. There are forms of anxiety that are caused by medical conditions like hyperthyroidism, hypoglycemia, cardiac arrhythmia and vitamin B12 deficiency. A doctor can help identify any medical conditions that may be contributing to your anxiety.

Pastoral Care

Pastoral care can be a gentle first step. Sometimes just talking with someone who listens, prays with you, and reminds you you're not alone makes a huge difference. It's not meant to replace professional help, but it can give you comfort, perspective, and a sense of community while you work through things.

Support from the Christian Community

I strongly encourage you to lean on trusted members of the Christian community when anxiety feels heavy. Sharing your struggles, praying together, and having people check in on you can ease the burden. Sometimes just knowing others care and stand with you makes things feel more manageable.

Scriptures for Breaking Free

The following are scriptures addressing fear and anxiety. I encourage you to read through all of them and select the ones that speak life into your situation. Take the ones you have selected and read them aloud over yourself daily - print them out and tape them to your bathroom mirror, put them in your wallet or purse, tape them to the back of the door of your home, tape them to the horn on your car, put them in the cover of your Bible, tape them to the edge of your computer monitor.

1. Genesis 15:1
2. Genesis 21:17
3. Genesis 26:24
4. Genesis 35:17
5. Genesis 43:23
6. Genesis 46:3
7. Genesis 50:19
8. Exodus 20:20
9. Deuteronomy 1:21
10. Deuteronomy 20:3
11. Deuteronomy 31:8
12. Joshua 8:1
13. Joshua 10:25
14. Judges 4:18
15. Judges 6:10
16. Judges 6:23
17. Ruth 3:11
18. Isaiah 4:20
19. Isaiah 12:20

20. Isaiah 22:23
21. Isaiah 23:17
22. 2 Samuel 9:7
23. 1 Samuel 13:28
24. 1 Kings 17:13
25. 2 Kings 6:16
26. 2 Kings 17:34
27. 2 Kings 25:24
28. 1 Chronicles 28:20
29. 2 Chronicles 20:17
30. Psalm 55:19
31. Psalm 65:4
32. Isaiah 7:4
33. Isaiah 35:4
34. Isaiah 41:13
35. Isaiah 41:14
36. Isaiah 43:1
37. Isaiah 43:5
38. Isaiah 44:2
39. Isaiah 54:4
40. Jeremiah 40:9
41. Jeremiah 46:27
42. Lamentations 3:57
43. Daniel 10:12
44. Daniel 10:19
45. Zechariah 8:13
46. Malachi 3:5
47. Matthew 1:20
48. Matthew 10:28
49. Matthew 28:5
50. Luke 1:13

51. Luke 1:30
52. Luke 2:10
53. Luke 5:10
54. Luke 8:50
55. Luke 12:7
56. Luke 12:32
57. Luke 18:4
58. John 12:15
59. Acts 27:24
60. 1 Peter 2:18
61. Revelation 1:17

A Final Word

While driving to an auto parts swap meet a few days ago, I was driving along listening to music. The song "Still Waters" sung by Leanna Crawford began to play. The words were so poignant I have to share them with you:

"Anxiety hates Psalm 23, so just say it to yourself 'til you believe it." (Fuller, Leonard, & Crawford, 2024)

I cannot think of any better advice that I could share with you. I studied under a pastor 30 years ago who encouraged us to read scripture out loud to ourselves. The logic behind this is that you trust your own voice over any other voice that you hear. So reading the TRUTH out loud so you hear your own voice speaking it, makes it easier for you to latch on and believe. By planting the Word in our hearts and minds by memorizing scripture, it makes it available for the Holy Spirit to call it up in our memory.

So if you don't do anything else with anything I have shared in this book, read this scripture over and over until you have it memorized. Then when anxiety and fear raise their nasty little heads, and they will, say it to yourself.

"The Lord is my shepherd; I shall not want.

He maketh me to lie down in green pastures: he leadeth me beside the still waters.

He restoreth my soul: he leadeth me in the paths of righteousness for his name's sake.

Yea, though I walk through the valley of the shadow of death, I will fear no evil: for thou art with me; thy rod and thy staff they comfort me.

Thou preparest a table before me in the presence of mine enemies: thou anointest my head with oil; my cup runneth over.

Surely goodness and mercy shall follow me all the days of my life: and I will dwell in the house of the Lord forever."
Psalm 23 KJV

Bibliography

10 Quotes from Billy Graham on Fear. (2020, March 17). Retrieved November 16, 2025, from Billy Graham Library: https://billygrahamlibrary.org/blog-10-quotes-from-billy-graham-on-fear/

Anxiety Disorders Treatment Market Sizing. (2025, March 27). Retrieved June 23, 2025, from Towards Healthcare: https://www.towardshealthcare.com/insights/anxiety-disorders-treatment-market-sizing

Delany, D. J. (2025, May 5). *How to Deal With Anxiety.* Retrieved July 7, 2025, from Ramsey Solutions: https://www.ramseysolutions.com/personal-growth/how-to-deal-with-anxiety

Fear: Merriam-Webster. (n.d.). Retrieved June 23, 2025, from Merriam-Webster: https://www.merriam-webster.com/

Fuller, B., Leonard, D., & Crawford, L. (Composers). (2024). Still Waters (Psalm 23). [L. Crawford, Performer]

Howard, L. (2023, May 10). *Anxiety disorders will affect nearly 1 in 3 adults: Here's what you need to know.* Retrieved 11 9, 2025, from UC Davis Health: https://health.ucdavis.edu/news/headlines/anxiety-disorders-will-affect-nearly-1-in-3-adults-heres-what-you-need-to-know/2023/05

Lewis, C. (2001). *Mere Christianity.* HarperOne.

Mental Health Information, Statistics, Any Anxiety Disorder. (n.d.). Retrieved 11 9, 2025, from National Institute of Mental Health: https://www.nimh.nih.gov/health/statistics/any-anxiety-disorder#part_2579

Also Available:

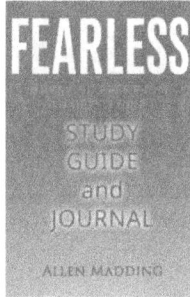

FEARLESS: Study Guide and Journal

Fearless: Breaking Free From Anxiety's Grip is more than a book—it's a companion for transformation.

This study guide offers reflective questions designed to deepen your journey from fear to faith, helping you move from anxiety's hold to the confidence of a conqueror.

To support lasting growth, a 12-month weekly journal is included, giving you space to record insights, victories, and prayers as you walk step by step into freedom.

Available from Amazon.com

Other Books by Allen Madding

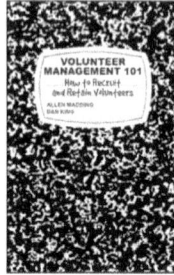

Volunteer Management 101:
How to Recruit and Retain Volunteers
by Allen Madding and Dan King

An employee needs the paycheck to pay the rent, the mortgage, the car payment, student debt, the credit card bill, the utilities, and a host of other bills. Volunteers, on the other hand are not motivated by a paycheck to stick it out when the manger is chewing someone out or things get uncomfortable.

The volunteer is simply motivated by making a difference and being a part of the organization. Their commitment hinges on how vested they are with the vision and purpose of the organization. When it gets to be too much of a hassle to serve, when they feel unappreciated, or when they feel the commitment is too demanding, they will walk away – usually without any warning or explanation.

With several decades of experience between them, Madding and King share insights on how to manage these valuable resources in your organization.

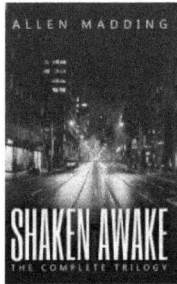

Shaken Awake: The Complete Trilogy
by Allen Madding

A dreadful chill ravages the city and a homeless man is found frozen to death on the church steps…

The city of Atlanta had weathered a thousand wet and chilly days in winter with occasional snowfall… but never one like this. A snowfall that begins in the noon turns into a vicious ice storm by evening, obliterating everything in its way. People are stuck into the whiteout, and trying to look for a way out.

Now, as the Peachtree Church opens its door to those out in cold, the church members come face to face with a stark reality.

As uncomfortable truths make themselves known, this storm will prove be to an eye opener for many.

Enlightening and compelling, Shaken Awake brings to surface a truth we either ignore or just don't know. With richly textured characters, haunted by the memories of their past, Shaken Awake is both a deeply engrossing novel and a thought-provoking piece of social commentary.

About the Author

Allen Madding is a passionate advocate for families, children, the hungry, and the homeless. A devoted follower of The Way, he serves as a house church pastor, while also pursuing his callings as an author, grant writer, and traveler. Beyond his ministry and writing, Allen is an enthusiastic fan of the Atlanta Braves, Georgia Southern University Eagles, Texas Longhorns, and Dallas Cowboys. Professionally, he works in information technology and makes his home in Thomasville, Georgia, with his wife, Allison.

He is a proud graduate of Georgia Southern University, where he earned a Bachelor of Business Administration in Management Information Systems, and Keller Graduate School of DeVry University, where he completed his Master of Business Administration.

www.ingramcontent.com/pod-product-compliance
Lightning Source LLC
LaVergne TN
LVHW051429080426
835508LV00022B/3309